D1064222

THE AGE OF CHIVALRY

English Society 1200-1400

SYLVIA WRIGHT

KINGFISHER
IN ASSOCIATION WITH
THE ROYAL ACADEMY OF ARTS

Contents

This book has been published in association with The Royal Academy of Arts for the *Age of Chivalry* exhibition sponsored by Lloyds Bank.

First published in 1987 by Kingfisher Books Limited, Elsley House, 24–30 Great Titchfield Street, London W1P 7AD, a Grisewood and Dempsey Company, in association with The Royal Academy of Arts, Piccadilly, London W1V 0DS.

BRITISH LIBRARY CATALOGUING IN PUBLICATION DATA
Wright, Sylvia
    The Age of Chivalry: English Society, 1200-1400
    1. Great Britain – History – 13th century –
    Juvenile literature 2. Great Britain – History
    – 14th century – Juvenile literature
    I. title II. Hook, Richard III. Royal
    Academy of Arts
    942.03   DA225
    ISBN 0-86272-318-3

Edited by Deborah Manley
Designed by Ben White
Printed in Belgium

Photographic Acknowledgments

The publishers and author wish to thank the following for kindly supplying photographs for this book:

Page 3 Cambridge University Library; 4 *top* British Library, *bottom* National Portrait Gallery; 5 *top* British Library, *bottom* British Library; 6 Bodleian; 11 D.O.E.; 12 *top* Philip Dunn, *bottom* V & A; 14 British Museum; 15 *top* V & A, *bottom* Northampton County Council; 16 Arthur Percival; 17 Faversham Town Council/Brian Hawkes; 18 Trinity College Library Dublin; 19 *top* Bristol Records Office, *bottom* Manchester City Art Gallery; 21 British Museum; 22 The Royal Library Copenhagen; 23 British Library; 24 V & A; 25 Bibliotheque Royale Albert Ier, Bruxelles; 26 Mervyn Blatch; 27 Ben White; 28 *top* Mervyn Blatch, *bottom* Woodmansterne; 29 Woodmansterne; 30 Sonia Halliday; 31 *top* The Cathedral Church of St Peter Exeter, *bottom* Cambridge University Library; 32 *left* Fitzwilliam Museum, *right* Woodmansterne; 34 *top* British Library, *bottom* Corpus Christi College Cambridge; 35 *top* Bibliothèque Mazarine Paris, *bottom* St Johns College, Oxford; 36 *top* Bodleian, *bottom* British Library; 38 Bibliothèque Royale Albert Ier, Bruxelles.

Picture Research Penny Warn and Lisa Simmons

Cover photograph: a page from the Ramsey Psalter, used by kind permission of Herr Abt Bruno Rader of St Paul's Austria.

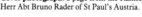

Power and People

Kingship

The medieval English king was not only the most powerful lord in the land: he was God's representative on Earth as well. The Coronation ceremony, in which he was not merely crowned and enthroned but also anointed with holy oil like a priest, was a dramatic expression of this link with divinity. His Coronation robes, which were encrusted with jewels, even made him look like a priest – a wonder-working priest from the Old Testament.

The English king too could perform wonders: his touch could cure the King's Evil, a glandular swelling now known as scrofula. Furthermore he had a saint, Edward the Confessor, among his forebears. Until Louis IX of France was made a saint in 1297, England was the only western European country with such a distinction in its royal family.

If he could bring health, the king could, with much greater certainty, bring death to subjects who displeased him. He was the source of law and justice. He was also the ultimate owner of all the territory he ruled, and the governor of the country. However, the country was large, its administration complex, and its inhabitants not always dutiful.

According to a medieval fable, society was like the human body. Its head was the king, the working people were its feet, and the soldiers and government officials were its hands. The king, in other words, had to delegate authority to others, and he was dependent on the cooperation of his subjects.

The image was worked out in great detail in the Middle Ages: the eyes are the justices, the heart the King's Council, the soul is the clergy, and the stomach represents the financiers. Sometimes the 'feet' object to carrying the apparently useless 'stomach', but, of course, each part is dependent upon all the others. Nevertheless, the head is always at the top, the feet will always be at the bottom, and every other member has its unalterable place.

A diagrammatic image of medieval society: monasteries and parishes are represented as Gothic tracery enclosed within the all-embracing arch of Papal power under Christ. Alphabetical characters stand for the people signified: those at the bases of the arcades indicate the Three Estates and *V(iri)* and *F(eminae)*, the men and women of the Middle Ages.

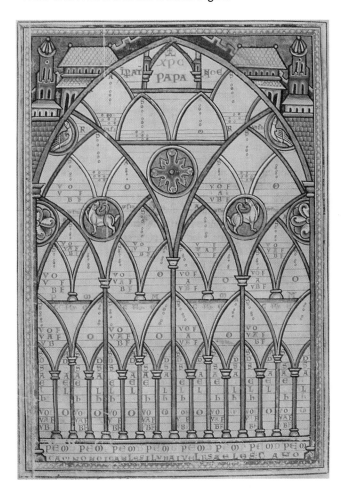

King John's enduring unpopularity with the clergy is reflected in this small picture (left) from a chronicle made about 1300, 85 years after his death. Here, a monk from Canterbury offers him poison. When John refused the Pope's appointment of an archbishop, he was excommunicated and all the churches in the land were closed.

Richard II sits enthroned holding the orb and sceptre, symbols of his power. This large panel painting (2.13 x .92m) showing him full length, was made about 1390, several years before Richard was deposed by his cousin Henry. It was probably painted from life, and is the earliest surviving portrait of an English monarch.

Countering this organized and organic emblem of society was the real world in which kings were incompetent or worse, and failed to realize that, although they were superior to their subjects, they were still dependent on their good will. Thus Edward II and Richard II lost the throne and their lives.

Being a king could be a dangerous as well as a difficult task. He was entrusted with enormous powers for one important reason: so that he could protect the people. They in turn paid him rent for the privilege of holding land, did 40 days military service a year, and paid special taxes in time of war. If a king abused his power or neglected his duty, the people had the right to replace him and give their allegiance to another lord.

In the thirteenth and fourteenth centuries, the kings had continually to defend themselves against rebellions, lest the body politic should receive a new head.

Magna Carta guarantees feudal rights to freemen and is still basic to the constitution of English law. King John was forced to sign it in 1215 and afterwards it was customary for all monarchs to reaffirm it. It is written in Latin. Here, Clause 39 reads: ''No free man shall be seized or imprisoned or stripped of his rights or possessions or outlawed or exiled or deprived of his standing in any other way. Nor will we proceed against him, or send others to do so except by the law of the land.'' These rights did not apply to peasants or to women.

Parliament

The system of representative government which we have today originated during the thirteenth century. Starting with King John, kings acknowledged that if they were to obtain the money they needed, they must include the barons in the decision making.

Both John and Henry III summoned assemblies of knights, elected by the 37 counties, to discuss financial aid. In 1265, during the Barons' Revolt of Simon de Montfort, representatives from the towns were also included. This gave wider support to the new kind of government. Edward I saw the wisdom of a large, unified assembly, and added representatives of the Church in the so-called 'Model Parliament' of 1295. The name 'parliament', which was in general use by the end of the thirteenth century, comes from a French word meaning 'discussion' or 'debate'.

During the fourteenth century, Parliament became much more than a debating society. It assumed responsibility from the king for organizing military affairs. The feudal army, composed of men serving their obligatory 40 days duty, was inadequate for long and expensive wars abroad. Parliament acquired the power to levy taxes and keep a regular army under the indenture system, whereby soldiers were contracted to serve for an agreed time or

Front and back of the seal of King John from the Magna Carta. Wax seals made from moulds owned by individuals had the legal force of a signature when affixed to documents. At first only the King had the right to use a seal, but by the thirteenth century anyone could own them.

objective. A 'House of Commons' came into being, including country gentry and wealthy merchants.

By the end of the century, Parliament was an organization of considerable power. When in 1397 Richard II tried to ignore its rights, the enraged barons deposed him. But still, Parliament met only at the King's discretion and he and his advisers decided what would be discussed. In addition, there still remained a large part of society which was not represented in the government at all.

The Medieval View of History

In the Middle Ages writers of history told a story of a universe which was created and organized by God. History proved that the physical world of nature and the social world of humanity conform to divine law. It was not an account of the events themselves, but a demonstration of how events reflect God's plan for humanity as it was known from the Bible. Events were interpreted in ways which seem strange today, but were seen by medieval scholars to have more important and deeper spiritual meanings. God's constant presence was to be understood as the highest truth to which all other facts must conform.

Chroniclers, on the other hand, compiled records which report current events year by year. At first these were only kept in monasteries, which were often isolated and more concerned with local history, but news from afar would be noted whenever it arrived.

Matthew Paris was the outstanding historian of the thirteenth century. He spent most of his life writing history and chronicles at St Albans where he lived as a monk. One of his most important books is *The Greater Chronicle* which records all history from the Creation to 1259, the year of his death. The record of events for the period after 1236, when he started to write from his own experience, provides a wealth of reliable information. Matthew's interests were wide ranging. He describes works of art and architecture about which, since they no longer exist, we would otherwise know nothing.

We know that he was acquainted with Henry III, but this did not stop him expressing his own views on the monarchy. He thought that Henry was extravagant and wasteful, and did not mince his words in saying so.

Other types of chronicles reflect the growing importance of towns. The Chronicle of the Mayors and Sheriffs of London provides much useful information about weights and measures and the problems of punishing merchants who cheat their customers.

Ranulph Higden, a monk from Chester, wrote his "Polychronicon" (Multiple History) in the mid-fourteenth century. He was a learned man whose horizons stretched far beyond his monastery. His theory of universal history was among the first to account for differences of geography, time, systems of governments and social customs.

Jean Froissart, who wrote in French, recounted the downfall of Richard II and the wars in France. His description of personalities greatly enriched the tradition of recording history.

Until the fourteenth century, histories were written in Latin, the language of the Church and scholars, but lay, or ordinary, people preferred the language which they spoke, so many of the histories were translated into English. From this time the running of the government and the business of ordinary people relied increasingly on written documents.

Brutus, legendary first King of Britain, departs from Greece. Later the goddess Diana appears to him in a dream to tell him that he will found a second Troy on an island beyond the setting sun. These pictures come from a chronicle of about 1300 from St Mary's Abbey, York.

SOCIAL AND POLITICAL EVENTS	FAITH	KNOWLEDGE

KING JOHN 1199-1216.

1208-1209 Pope excommunicates King John and all English churches are closed.

1210 St Francis of Assisi founds Franciscan Order of Friars.

1211 St Dominic founds Dominican Order of Friars.

1215 Magna Carta.

1215 Fourth Lateran Council in Rome establishes standards of pastoral care.

HENRY III 1216-1272.
1217 Forest Charter begins to open
up forest lands.

1221 First friars come to England: influence on religious life, learning and society.

1222 Council of Oxford: parish priests to be better educated.

1235 Robert Grosseteste appointed Bishop of Lincoln.

c.1235 Encyclopedic summaries of religion, science and law begun by Alexander
of Hales, Bartholomew the Englishman and Henry Bracton.

1245 King commissions rebuilding of Westminster Abbey in emulation of Louis IX of France, and introduces concepts of royal
church and architectural structure new to England.

1258 The Barons' Revolt.
1265 Simon de Montfort's Parliament.

1266-67 Roger Bacon's 'Opus majus'
advances experimental science optics and
calendar reform.

1269 Edward the Confessor
enshrined in Westminster Abbey.

EDWARD I 1272-1307.
1276 Campaign in Wales; Welsh
castles built.

1277 Roger Bacon exiled for
heresy.
1281 Council of Lambeth: laymen to receive systematic religious education.

1284 Wales becomes English colony.
1290 Expulsion of the Jews.
1295 The 'Model' Parliament.

c.1300 First mechanical clock.

1304 Conquest of Scotland.
1305 Robert the Bruce rebels.

1300 Pre-eminence of Oxford theologians and philosophers
(Duns Scotus, Thomas Bradwardine, William of Ockham etc)

EDWARD II 1307-1327.
1314 English defeat at Bannockburn.
1315-17 Crop failures and famine.
1327 Edward II deposed.

1324 William of Ockham charged with
heresy

1320-35 Thomas Bradwardine at Oxford
applies mathematics to scientific theory.

EDWARD III 1327-1377

c.1330 Ranulf Higden begins his
'Polychronicon'.
1337 First scientific weather records by
William Merlee in Oxford.

1337 Edward declares himself King
of France. 100 Years War begins.
1340 Only Parliament can impose taxes.

1349 The Black Death appears in Dorset coastal town; by end of 1350 one third of the population of England has died.

1349 English taught instead of French in
schools.

1351 Statute of Labourers to hold
wages and prices down.

c.1357 'Lay-Folks' Catechism' offers
religious instruction in English
verse (based on Council of Lambeth).

1362 King addresses Parliament in English.

1362 English is to be used in the law courts.

1370 *Piers Plowman* written by William Langland.
1373 Julian of Norwich writes
Revelations of Divine Love.

1376 The 'Good' Parliament
and death of the Black Prince.

1370 Froissart begins his chronicles in
French.

RICHARD II 1377-1399.
1381 The Peasants' Revolt.
1398 Henry Bolingbroke exiled.
1399 Henry Bolingbroke returns.
Richard is deposed.

1380s The Bible is first translated into English. Lollard persecution begins.

1387-1400 Chaucer's *Canterbury Tales.*

HENRY IV 1399-1413.

1399 John Trevisa translates Bartholomew
The Englishman into English.

Three Estates

Medieval society considered itself to be divided into three estates, or classes, based on professions: those who pray, those who fight and those who work. Everyone took his place in this world at birth; and, since it was God's will that humanity should be divided in this way, social climbing was frowned upon. The poor were expected not to be envious and the rich were taught to pity those less fortunate than themselves.

Various writers attempted to justify this rigid system. In the *Book of St Albans*, for example, its origins go back to the first family. Adam and Eve had three sons, each different in character. Cain, a farmer, killed his brother Abel out of jealousy, so God condemned him to a life of poverty and wandering: no matter how hard he worked, he would always be poor, an outcast and a symbol of Evil. Seth, the surviving son, was fortunate enough to have heirs and, through them, founded a race of nobility: superiority was justified by virtue.

In practice, people could and did better their circumstances or even fall from grace. By the thirteenth century, the feudal hierarchy was already crumbling. Fighting was no longer required of the nobility and even a successful farmer could buy a place in high society. Learning, once the exclusive province of the clergy, was opened up to others. Expanding

This picture of the late-medieval social hierarchy is based upon manuscript illustrations. Status in society is indicated both by position and by scale (or relative size). The first estate, the clergy, is at the top: a bishop, a priest, a nun, a monk and a Dominican friar. A noble family represents the second estate: a knight and his squire (or apprentice), the lady and the children.

trade provided the means for merchants to rise from the class of workers to the nobility.

On the other hand, landless knights roamed the country in search of a lord and often lived in poverty despite their good breeding. Many journeymen, or trained craftsmen, could not obtain the tenancy on property they required to become masters, and so had to work for others.

Some people, like Jews or foreigners, never fitted into the system at all. The Jews were even expelled from the country. Foreigners were regarded as enemies of the established guilds, or associations of craftsmen, and were therefore often denied the right to practise their trades.

The most glaring exclusion from the system is the estate of women. A woman's place in this world depended almost entirely on whom she married, regardless of which estate she was born into. By law she was excluded from government and its administration. Her legal rights were limited. The women who prayed, the nuns, could never administer the Sacrament, nor other rites of the Church.

In the view of the Church the moral inferiority of women also went back to Eve. When she took the apple against God's instructions and then lured Adam into eating it with her, she committed the Original Sin. It was her fault that humanity was excluded from Paradise.

The bottom two rows are the third estate, where the vast majority of people would have fitted in. Those who have risen to the middle class are a scholar, a lawyer, a palmer, a goldsmith, a freeman and a merchant. The unfree people and the foot soldiers on the bottom row represent the members of society who worked the land and were dependent upon or obligated to an overlord.

Those Who Fight

The Aristocracy

Those who fight, the knights, became the main land-holders or barons. They were the over-lords of most of the people. By the thirteenth century this class of people were not necessarily warriors. In place of military service a noble could offer 'scutage', a payment in money. Status could now be purchased. A man who was successful in farming or education, or excelled in service to a lord, could move up the social ladder. One of the best ways to do this was to marry a wealthy heiress. Land and titles were inherited. Usually the eldest son was given the lot; younger sons had to make their own way, and often entered the clergy. If there were no sons, the daughters divided the inheritance. There was a great demand for these wealthy heiresses and they tended to marry very young. In Essex in the early thirteenth century, the rich young Galiena de Damartin was only seven years old when she married for the first time.

As wealth increased in the kingdom so did the standard of living of the upper class. As society moved away from feudalism, the kind of houses they lived in also changed. In the earlier medieval period the great lords in all parts of the country had to design houses that could be defended. These not only provided accommodation for themselves, but for their troops as well. Castles were usually built on high ground so that any approaching enemy could be seen

Caernafon Castle, seen here from the north, was built as a royal seat and memorial to past imperial power: Magnus Maximus, father of the Emperor Constantine, was buried here. The polygonal turrets, and bands of coloured masonry, and eagles on top of triple turrets at the principal towers imitate the land walls of Constantinople. The castle is about 200 metres long, the Eagle Tower is about 22 metres in diameter. The King's Gate, centre, had six portcullises and five double doors. Inside are two baileys.

from a distance. Stone walls were built to surround them and these were often protected by a ditch called a motte.

The inhabitants spent most of their time in a great hall inside the castle walls, but retreated to a tower, or keep, in times of siege. As feudalism declined, the need for military design in houses decreased and fortified manor houses began to replace castles. These had thinner walls, larger windows and were increasingly designed for comfort.

The ten new castles built in North Wales by Edward I between 1272 and 1307, such as Caernafon, Conway and Denbigh, show feudal castle design at its most developed. The wars in Wales were close enough to home to be fought by knights serving their 40 days duty, and these were the last great castles to be built for feudal warfare. They take maximum advantage of the longbow. At Caernafon, for example, the south side of the exterior castle wall was made extra high, and long, narrow windows were arranged in three tiers so that three times as many archers could shoot at once.

The Investiture Ceremony (above) is a twentieth-century addition to royal pageanty. The Investiture of the Prince of Wales at Caernafon Castle in 1969 was designed both to win over Welsh nationalists and to promote the popularity of the monarchy. Prince Charles was crowned by the Queen and swore a feudal oath. He then gave a speech in Welsh and was presented at the main gates of the castle.

Heraldry

By the end of the twelfth century the knight donned protective armour so all-concealing that on horseback he was scarcely recognizable. With his entire body covered in chain mail, and a surcoat worn over that, plus a helmet on top, it was extremely difficult to distinguish whether he was friend or foe on the battlefield.

To solve this vital problem, warriors began to wear their individual personal insignia, or arms, on their shields. The term 'coat of arms' comes from the custom of painting arms on the linen surcoats. With the passing of time these emblems came to be recognized as signs of important families. They represented status and pride in noble birth.

In later centuries, when actual fighting became less important to a man's claim to position, the coat of arms served to identify knights in the mock battles which were a favourite pastime of the nobility. The owners wore them on horse trappings, helmets and crests, and they decorated their personal possessions with them. When used on seals, they added a touch of pride and honour to the legal

The brilliance of stained glass is an excellent medium for heraldic colours. Here a shield with the arms of John of Gaunt, fourth son of Edward III (from St Peter's Church, Witherley, Leicestershire) is being restored. The combined arms of England and France are further combined with the arms of Castile (*gules a castle or*) and Leon (*argent a lion rampant sable*). These were Spanish areas which came to John of Gaunt through marriage.

The lid of this silver-gilt casket (shown actual size) made between 1299 and 1307 bears the arms of England (three leopards) and France (lilies) representing the marriages of Edward I and the future Edward II to French princesses. The crested lid and the windows on the sides imitate a building.

signature. Eventually, having the entitlement to bear arms replaced knighthood as the entry into high society.

There seem to have been strict rules for the design of coats of arms in England as early as 1255, and these are still in use today. Heraldry, or the design of arms, even has its own special language called *blazon*. Only seven colours can be used: *azur* (blue), *gules* (red), *vert* (green), *sable* (black), and *purpur* (purple) and two metallic colours: *or* (gold) and *argent* (silver). Very few patterns and types of objects and beasts are permitted. The French origin of the words emphasizes the dependency of the aristocratic circles on French fashions.

As heraldry increased in complexity and status, the position of the people who knew all about it also rose. The first function of these 'heralds' was to announce the identity of knights at tournaments. In the fourteenth century there was a practical need for a lord to have someone around him who could identify shields, and heralds were often retained at court. Their duties came to include registration of the promotions to knighthood and some even became diplomats.

Knights

Like the king, the knight had the job of protecting the Church and the people. The vital difference was that the knight had to do it physically; he was a professional fighting man. As such he was often brutal and callous, but the ideal of knighthood embodied spiritual values scarcely less elevated than those of kingship.

The knight went through a formal initiation ceremony, which in fact influenced Coronation ritual; and he too was invested with symbolic regalia. This was his armour, regarded as an emblem of his virtues. His shield was faith, his helmet hope, and his sword the word of God. The idea came from a passage in St Paul's Epistle to the Ephesians, but it was greatly extended in the Middle Ages, and included the knight's horse, which was goodwill: its saddle represented Christianity, the saddlecloth humility and so on.

The original English knight before the Norman Conquest had no need for horse-trappings. He was a foot soldier, a young man who owed military service to his lord (the Anglo-Saxon word *cniht* means simply 'youth'). The idea of a knight as a mounted warrior comes from the French concept of chivalry and the *chevalier* or horseman. Since horses and their equipment were expensive, this new kind of knight was by definition a wealthy man, and hence the title came to be associated with social rank as well as skill at arms.

Despite – or perhaps because of – his violent life-style, the knight was a hero in the medieval world. Literature glorified his role, the Church blessed it, and society regarded it as the ultimate expression of an ethical code that was second in influence only to religion: chivalry.

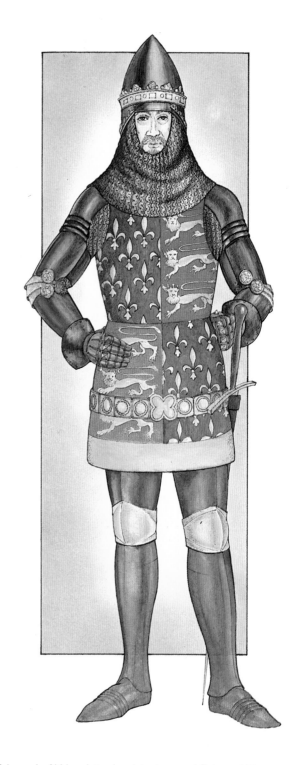

Edward of Woodstock, eldest son of Edward III, was called the Black Prince because of his black armour. Military successes abroad made him a national hero and poets praised his virtue. Yet he was responsible for atrocities which are appalling even by medieval standards. When the city of Limoges defected to the French in 1370, he burned it to the ground and killed the entire population of over 3000.

Chivalry

Throughout the Middle Ages, commentators complained that the Age of Chivalry was dead. Chivalric conduct represented an ideal that was easier to achieve in literature than in life, and it is in the Arthurian Romances rather than in historical events that we find chivalry in action. However, chivalry as defined in handbooks of instruction for knights was no fiction: it was an attempt to establish a code of behaviour suited to contemporary society. Like that society, it was complex and sometimes contradictory.

The fundamentals of chivalry were that the knight must defend not only the Christian Faith and the king, but also the weak and oppressed: he was an embodiment of justice. From these duties arose personal qualities. To be an effective defender, the knight must be brave and practised in arms. As a soldier of God, he must be pious and pure in heart. Defence of the weak meant he must be generous in his charity; it also came increasingly to mean fighting on behalf of a lady, and chivalry developed a strong romantic element.

All these factors are combined in a popular medieval moral tale. Here Christ is portrayed as a knight who rescues his bride, the human soul, from his enemy, the Devil. The knight dies

In the earlier Middle Ages Christian soldiers joined the Crusades to the Holy Land to defend the Church. Richard the Lion Heart's victory over Saladin of Egypt symbolizes the Church's triumph over Evil. It is depicted here on two tiles of about 1260 made at Chertsey Abbey in Surrey.

from his wounds, but his widow remains faithful to him and preserves his blood-stained armour in her chamber. In other words, the soul keeps faith in the crucified Christ. While the moralizing message is typical of medieval storytelling, the mixture of violence, religion, love and loyalty is essentially chivalric rather than devout.

Reality was less clear-cut than the story of the Christ-knight. The need to reconcile warfare and Christianity, purity and amorous exploits, were problems to tax the most devious medieval thinkers. The answer was to impose a set of conventions on knightly conduct. War was formalized into the tournament: a disciplined armed conflict fought with all the panoply of battle but without, in theory, its bloodshed. Tournaments and their single-combat equivalents, jousts, were not merely martial exercises; they were also spectator sports, and opportunities for the knight to display his prowess.

Romance, too, acquired a set of rules for the

pursuit of so-called 'courtly love', though this was also probably more of theoretical than practical application. It involved long courtship and impeccable behaviour from the knight, who was to be utterly devoted to his lady.

The story of Sir Lancelot and Queen Guinevere illustrates courtly love in action. Lancelot, King Arthur's bravest knight, sets out to deliver his adored Guinevere from an abductor. He undergoes a series of adventures, at one of which he hesitates. He rescues Guinevere, but she learns about his hesitation and makes him go through a further round of ordeals before surrendering to him. The significance of the story is not merely that love is supreme, to be pursued unswervingly at whatever cost, but also that Guinevere is Arthur's wife: courtly love is more important even than marriage.

Chivalrous behaviour stressed loyalty and generosity as well as romance and valour. Generosity in warfare is exemplified by the treatment of prisoners: ransom, or even parole, was offered to defeated survivors of battle. In peacetime it is demonstrated by the alms and gifts the knight bestows. The Black Prince, despite his savage conduct, was notable for clemency to captives and generosity to friends.

Medieval critics may have felt that the true Age of Chivalry was to be found in the days of King Arthur, but, for all its imperfections, the chivalric ideal of the thirteenth and fourteenth centuries was a powerful social code that has continued to shape our ideas about civilized behaviour.

Romance also had a practical side: landless knights who would otherwise be without income could better their fortunes by securing a position with a wealthy patron. The lady on the silver Bermondsey Dish (top right) accepts the devotion offered by a knight.

Loyalty within marriage is nowhere more publicly demonstrated than by the Eleanor Crosses Edward I erected in memory of his wife. Twelve crosses marked the resting places of her bier along the journey from Lincoln to London. Only the death of St Louis of France had been so ostentatiously commemorated before. The Hardingstone Cross in Northamptonshire (right) was sculpted in the new ornate Decorated style by John of Battle and William of Ireland in 1291-2.

Those Who Work

Towns, Villages and Cities

Between 1227 and 1250 more than 12,000 settlements in England and Wales acquired market rights from the king. Although many of these places never grew into towns, this fact is evidence of the growth of local trade. Some of the settlements were probably nothing more than places where fairs were held one week of the year, but many others grew into real towns.

Market towns centre on a market place and church. They often develop along main roads or trade routes. Market stalls become shops and then houses are built around the open market place or along the single main street, so traders are near the stream of customers who come to town to buy their wares. This kind of town often has no walls for defence. Many other towns grew up under the protection of castles, originating in the need to house those who served the lord of the castle.

Town customs varied widely. Southampton, for instance, was governed by the Merchant Guild; Beverly was run by twelve 'Keepers' selected from the most distinguished citizens. At Bury St Edmunds the monks of the monastery chose a 'Bailiff' who ran the town.

Foreign trade was also expanding and towns with ports, like Bristol, became very wealthy. Bristol grew to be the third largest town in the country. London is estimated to have been three times the size of York, the next most populous centre, but there is no sure way of telling the exact populations.

About thirty towns in England, like Faversham in Kent, shown here, were attached to monasteries or abbeys. Above, the Guildhall in present day Faversham occupies a prominent place in the town.

Faversham Horn

The use of the horn as a signal on the hunting-field has survived to the present. Its corresponding role as a call to attention in civic affairs has lapsed, but during the Middle Ages these ancient and simple musical instruments were used to summon free men to elect their officials. The Faversham Horn is signed by its maker, Richard Young, and is made of latten, a kind of brass, and covered in leather. It was made about 1300.

Merchants and Craftsmen

It has been estimated that about 5 per cent of the population in the towns – the burgesses – controlled about 40 per cent of the property. These individuals held land under a system of rent called *burgage* which meant that no services were required of them, they simply paid rent to their landlord.

Within the towns these wealthier merchants formed guilds, or associations which regulated trade and protected it from outsiders. In many towns the guilds also ran the local government: they formed the council and chose their own mayor. The middle classes, perhaps a half or more of the total population, and the poor were sometimes left out of government entirely.

The merchants were the middlemen. They bought goods produced in the countryside and sold them to the townspeople. The major source of income and wealth was wool. Those who sold it for export found a profitable

Matthew Paris's *Life of St Alban* of about 1250 provides evidence of medieval building technique. Two bricklayers check the wall: one uses a level, the other a plumb-line. A workman operates a windlass and pulley to lift a basket of stones. In the foreground a stone mason carves a capital with an adze. In front of him are a hammer and set-square. A carpenter, right, squares a piece of wood and another bores a hole with an auger into a scaffolding pole.

market. The best overseas customer was Flanders, where the weavers made it into fine cloth. Grain, cheese, metals, and hides were also in demand abroad.

The goods which came into the country from the Continent suggest that many people enjoyed a luxurious life style. Fine silks and cloth of gold were imported from Italy; Flemish cloth and French wine were also sold in England.

Many people who set up business in the town were involved in the manufacture of goods.

Craftsmen also formed guilds. These developed at different rates throughout the country and, on the whole, were slower to form than were the merchant guilds. In the thirteenth century they were already an established feature of life in the cities, but in many country towns they were only just beginning to emerge.

Master craftsmen controlled the quality of all goods produced and the prices charged for them, and they also decided who could practise the trade.

In order to become a professional craftsman, such as a blacksmith, baker or weaver, a person had to serve an apprenticeship which could last as long as seven years. Boys had to find a master who was willing to train them and they had to pass an exam at the end of the training. Then, in order to run a shop, they had to find a building and acquire a tenancy. Not everyone who passed the final examination was guaranteed work at the end of it, yet the length of the training made it very difficult for a craftsman to change profession.

However guilds were much more than just clubs for businessmen and women. They not only protected the trades, they also assumed a spiritual, social and economic responsibility for the welfare of members. Each trade had a patron saint on whose feast day celebrations took place. Membership fees of the guilds were often used to help the sick and those who needed money. When a member died, the other guild members had a solemn duty to attend the funeral. In happier times the guilds provided entertainment, and on feast days and Holy Days put on religious plays.

A gold ring brooch set with garnets and sapphires (top right). This fine example of a medieval goldsmith's work was found recently in a Manchester street near some excavations.

The Bristol Charter of 1347 grants the city the right to imprison night walkers and punish fraudulent merchants. In the bottom picture in this illuminated initial (right), a baker is punished for selling short-weight loaves by being tied to a ladder and dragged through the streets.

Village and Countryside

The medieval landscape would have looked much like a patchwork quilt, made up of numerous small fields and large tracts of woodland. Country people lived in villages or hamlets: a cluster of houses and usually a church in the centre of arable land which was often cultivated by the open-field method. Each field was divided into uneven blocks and ploughed in strips by individual farmers. Cooperation between farmers was essential; everybody had to plant their crops at the same time, so they could be harvested at the same time. Teams of oxen were made up by farmers collectively, for it was rare for one person to own a whole team.

Providing food in winter was extremely difficult. Breeding animals were kept through the winter; the others were slaughtered for food. Much of the countryside was forested, but hunting in the king's forest was illegal, and reserved for the king's pleasure. This caused bitter resentment, not only amongst the peasants but also amongst other classes. Gradually Parliament forced the king to open up these lands, but it was a struggle.

While the open-field system was found in areas of Yorkshire, Lincolnshire, the Midlands and much of the south, other parts of the country, where animals were grazed, would have looked quite different. In areas such as

Kent, where sheep were reared, uncultivated pastureland was more common. Sheep were not bred for meat as they are now, but for their dung for fertilizer, milk for making cheese, and their skin, both for sheepskins and for making parchment for pages of books, but most importantly, of course, for their wool.

The life styles of people who worked the land varied from region to region. Within the village community, a tenant farmer could be either free or unfree. Workers might also be hired on a yearly basis by the lord of the manor, or even a wealthy tenant. By the end of the fourteenth century status in the community had more to do with a person's wealth than with his legal status. An unfree but well-to-do man's could be higher than his free but poorer neighbours.

The church and the manorial court were the most important centres of village social life. A court of elected jurors with the power to fine and punish wrongdoers helped to ensure everyone's best behaviour. Male tenants in groups of ten, called tithings, elected a chief tithingman who was responsible for reporting offences. However, writers of the time complain about the loose morals of the villagers: dancing in the churchyard, holding beauty contests, and hooliganism are cited as evidence. The parish priests, on the other hand, would have organized more wholesome entertainment such as pilgrimages to local shrines, celebrations on Holy Days and religious plays.

A modern artist has based this springtime sowing scene on pictures from the Psalter made for Sir Geoffrey Luttrell in the mid fourteenth century. About 90% of the population of late medieval England lived in the country, dependent upon the land for their livelihood. The prosperity of the thirteenth century was followed by crop failures and famine in the early fourteenth. After the Black Death of 1349-50 which killed one-third of the people, laws were passed which restricted wages and prices. In 1381 the farm workers' resentment exploded in the Peasants' Revolt.

Those Who Pray

Religion

The hold that religion had over people in the Middle Ages is almost unimaginable today. The power structure, centred on Rome, touched everyone. Even the King paid homage to his overlord the Pope.

The archbishops of Canterbury and York directed the Church in their regions. There were two main types of clergy: seculars who took care of the spiritual interests of the lay people, and the religious orders who were full-time worshippers, men and women who lived in monasteries and convents.

The parish priest played a vital role in the lives of ordinary people. He lived amongst them; baptized them when they came into the world; buried them in the churchyard when they left it. He often educated the children. In return, he was granted an extra strip of land and the people paid him tithes, a tenth of their assets. Alternatively a priest might be employed by the local monastery, in which case he would be paid a salary. The first sort of priest was called a vicar, the second a rector, and the terms survive to this day.

In the earlier Middle Ages the major concern of the Church was to save the world from the Infidel or unbelievers. The Church sponsored the Crusades, or Wars of the Cross, to recapture the Holy Land from the Moslems. Knights from all over Europe travelled to Jerusalem to defend the Christian faith.

In the thirteenth century, perhaps under the influence of the newly founded universities, the Church recognized a new enemy. The greatest threat to faith was now seen as ignorance, carelessness and greed. The Church began to look inwardly at itself and its people to identify the source of Evil.

A new approach was devised to combat these problems. It was decided that every individual had to confess all their sins at least once a year and priests became responsible, not only for determining penance, or punishment for sins, but for the spiritual guidance of their parishioners. Everyone had to learn a lot more, not only about sin, but about human nature too.

Books were written to teach all Christians about the virtues and vices. At first the virtues were treated like antidotes to poison, but later they came to be encouraged for their own sake. Thoughts and feelings became more elevated and spiritual as a result. Manuals for priests had instructions for the guidance of individuals according to their estates. Although both men and women were considered equally worthy of

The great reward Christianity offered was eternal paradise. Judgement Day, when Christ would return to establish his kingdom on Earth and resurrect the dead to decide their fates, was expected soon. Everyone who confessed and had done penance could look forward to a better world. Here, in a Psalter of about 1370 made for the wealthy Bohun family, are the Seven Penitential Psalms which were said for penance. They formed part of the services on Ash Wednesday in Lent and in the Coronation service, and were commonly illustrated by a Last Judgement.

mercy, women were treated separately with special considerations according to their status.

A new kind of religious person, the friar, began to come into England in the 1220s. Critical of the wealth and privilege of the traditional Church, the friars travelled about the country and begged for a living. Their purpose was to educate the people. People appreciated their poverty as an attempt to return to the ideas of Christ's disciples and they enjoyed their sermons as a popular kind of entertainment.

Another group, the Lollards, were also critical of the Church. Centering on the figure of John Wyclif, a fourteenth-century philosopher at Oxford, they attacked the worship of saints, pilgrimage, and the use of pictures as an aid to devotion. They wanted the Bible translated into English so that everyone could read it. Their most upsetting idea was that the communion wine and wafers were not the actual blood and flesh of Christ. They were excommunicated and many died for their beliefs.

The English mystics represent the extremes of striving for personal experience in religion. Mysticism is a state of prayer in which the worshipper's soul unites with God. Sometimes the mystic sees visions or hears voices. Julian of Norwich was a hermit who wrote about the sixteen 'showings' which she saw in 1373. In her book, *Revelations of Divine Love*, she describes the Passion of Christ which she saw as if she was one of the actual onlookers.

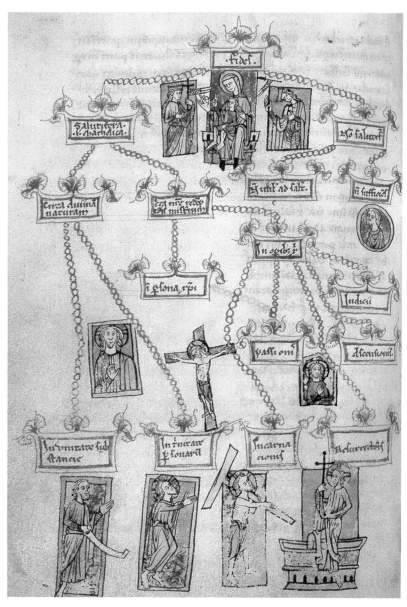

The Christian faith is set out as a diagram in an early thirteenth-century manuscript made at the Cistercian monastery of Abbey Dore in Herefordshire. The terms depend on the Parisian theologian Peter Abelard but the layout derives from sixth century teaching methods. It typifies the kind of educational aid that would have been used for religious instruction in medieval England. Faith is represented by the Virgin and Child at the top; they are flanked by female figures personifying the Church and the Synagogue. A network of chain-like lines leads the reader to labels and images that set out the faith that is inadequate (from Synagogue to the top right corner) and that which leads to Salvation (on the left and taking up most of the page). Complex ideas are simplified in verbal and visual terms. Lower left, pictures of a prophet and Christ in prayer represent the ideas of God as one substance and three persons, basic to the doctrine of the Trinity. Five connected labels, lower right, list essential points in the life of Christ: the Incarnation (God assuming human form), the Passion (Christ's painful death on the Cross), the Resurrection, the Ascension into Heaven, and finally Judgement.

Worship

Sunday Mass, the Church service most people attended, was conducted entirely in Latin, a language few could understand. Quite often the priest knew little Latin either and mumbled incoherently. There were complaints about the congregation "gossipping and fumbling."

One thing that would have been clear to everyone was the terrifying picture of Doom painted above the chancel arch. Here the constant threat of eternal damnation, which was the great hold the Church had over people, was exploited to the full. Naked souls of the Damned were tormented in Hell – hanging on burning trees or ripped apart by demons – while the Blessed, those who had confessed and done penance, were led off to eternal bliss in Heaven. Wandering attention might also focus on the large Crucifix – a reminder that Christ died to redeem sinful humankind.

In 1222 the Council of Oxford took measures to amend the shortcomings of the clergy, and by the end of the fourteenth century they were much better trained. But it was probably the friars who made the real drive for improvement.

In addition to the Sunday services there were many Holy Days throughout the year. In the Middle Ages no one had holidays (except for monks), so the days which commemorate events in the life of Christ and the anniversaries of the deaths of saints became the cause of more and bigger celebrations as the years went by. For each of these days a special Mass and prayers were said.

Devotion

A daily cycle of prayer and worship was observed by the religious orders of monks and nuns. The eight Hours of prayer, or Canonical Hours, were a sequence of services which began in the middle of the night. Matins and Lauds were combined, starting five hours before sunrise. The remaining six services were celebrated at intervals until early evening. Mass would also be said, before the Hour of Sext (midday). The intervening time was filled with work, meditation and reading.

In the later Middle Ages, literate lay people began to conduct private devotions. The book which they were recommended to read was the Psalter, the poetical book of Psalms from the Bible. This was also read in the monasteries as part of their observance.

As time went on a special book was devised for lay needs. The Book of Hours is based on the Canonical Hours which were observed in the cloisters. The services are shorter, and centred on events in the life of the Virgin Mary with other devotional texts. The most prominent feature of Books of Hours is their illustration and decoration. The narrative pictures of Gospel scenes provided matter for meditation, while the marginal ornament ensured that the reader's attention was concentrated on the page.

Only a few people could afford to own these books. Even wealthier people could also have private chaplains and chapels in their own homes, but most people had to be content with what the Church offered them.

This elaborately illuminated Psalter (right) was made before 1318 for the Abbot of Peterborough Abbey. Inside the initial 'B', King David, author of the Psalms, plays a harp with accompaniment from birds and musicians. In the margin a youthful David aims his sling at Goliath. Birds, animals, hunting scenes and grotesques (invented creatures) provide comic relief from the serious task of devotional reading.

This tiny (7.2 x 8.1 cm) portable triptych was used for private lay devotion. It was made about 1350 of gold and translucent enamel. St Christopher, the patron saint of travellers, and All Saints on the wings flank images of St Anne teaching the Virgin to read and the Visitation. The saints John the Baptist, James of Compestella, Edmund and Giles are identifiable by their costume or the objects they hold.

qui non abijt in consilio
impiorum et in uia pecca
torum non stetit: et in cathe
dra pestilentie non sedit.
Sed in lege domini uo
luntas eius: et in lege ei
meditabitur die ac nocte.
Et erit tamquam lig
num quod plantatum
est secus decursus aquarum:
quod fructum suum da
bit in tempore suo.
Et folium eius non de
fluet: et omnia quecum
que faciet prospabuntur.
Non sic impij non sic:
sed tamquam puluis
quem proicit uentus
a facie terre.
Ideo non resurgunt

impij in iudicio: neque pec
catores in consilio iustor.
Quoniam nouit dñs
uiam iustor: et iter im
piorum peribit.
Quare fremuerunt
gentes: et populi
meditati sunt
inania?
Astiterunt reges terre.
et principes conuenerut
in unum: aduersus dñm
et aduersus xpm eius.
Dirumpamus uincula
eorum: et piciamus a no
bis iugum ipsorum.
Qui habitat in celis ir
ridebit eos: et dominus
subsannabit eos.
Tunc loquetur ad eos
in ira sua: et in furore
suo conturbabit eos.
Ego autem constitutus
sum rex ab eo super syon
montem sanctum eius:
predicans preceptum eius.
Dominus dixit ad me
filius meus es tu: ego
hodie genui te.
Postula a me et dabo tibi
gentes hereditatem tuam

The Church

The village church was the heart of the manorial settlement. Its tower dominated the landscape and it was the finest building in the community. In the late Middle Ages, when many new churches were built, the average population of a parish was about 250. There were 8-12,000 churches in the country. The parish boundaries were strictly observed: a person could only attend services in his own parish, unless he was a friar, traveller or soldier going to battle.

The thirteenth-century bell tower came to be much taller than the rest of the church. It not only served as a symbol of the importance of religion in people's lives, but its bells summoned the people to services and signalled curfew at night when they were obliged to put out their fires. A typical church would have two or three bells. In the fourteenth century bell wheels replaced single-spindle bells.

The bells announced the beginning of Mass and the moment when the priest raised the chalice, or wine cup: the Elevation. Most bell towers had sundials with a notch for the hour of Mass marked in a heavier line.

The height of the church was further emphasized by the decorative and functional features of the rest of the building. The use of the chisel and gouge had made more refined carving possible. Fine stone tracery (the bars between window panes) allowed the windows to let in more light. Stone supports became taller and thinner. The sculptured decoration became more naturalistic and the amount of decoration increased.

As the worshippers entered the porch of the church they would pause briefly to dip their fingers into a stoup, or basin, filled with holy water, and then make the sign of the cross. The porch was used for religious functions; it also served as a courtroom and place of business.

All Saints Church in Bakewell, Derbyshire, like most parish churches, was built over many centuries. Fragments of sculpture survive from the ninth century and some of the walls and the west portal were built in the twelfth. The windows with two lancets and a pierced spandrel are Early English. Later Perpendicular windows have three panels and elaborate tracery. Bakewell's central belltower was begun in the thirteenth century. The 'Breach Spire', from the octagonal base upwards, was finished c.1340. Although parts of the building were replaced in the 19th century, the builders were careful to preserve the original style. The fourteenth century battlements across the top are also found on the funeral monument inside the church which is shown on the opposite page (top right). Also on the opposite page is a diagram showing the parts of a church. Another type of church plan has been used, with the belltower at one end.

Once inside the main body of the church, the nave, everyone had to stand. The weak or infirm could, if necessary, go to the wall, where they could support themselves. The open area of the nave was used for festival celebrations as well as church services. But, later in the fourteenth century, when preaching became more popular, seating and pulpits were built.

The roodscreen with its imposing Crucifix and the painted Doom on the wall above the chancel arch almost separated the people from the priest. The altar, the single most important thing in the church, was housed in the enclosed area of the chancel. The altar, the table which holds the items used in the celebration of the Mass ʰad five crosses marked on the top which repr   Christ's wounds. Behind the altar w   ʰeen a screen with either painted or ᵢmages of Christ's Passion.

The wall-tomb carved from alabaster in 1377 of Sir Godfrey Foljambe and his wife in Bakewell Church in Derbyshire with its upright, lively figures is not typical. The dead are usually portrayed recumbent. The canopied niche and embattled top create a stage-like setting similar to those used to frame figures of saints for the alabaster altar pieces which were, like this tomb, made in Nottingham near the quarries.

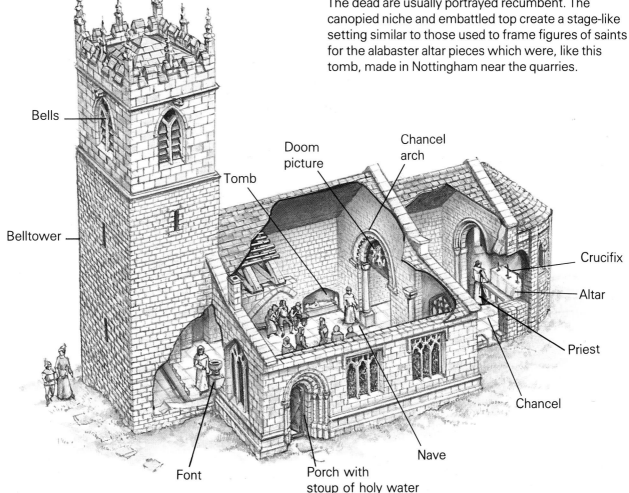

Bells

Belltower

Tomb

Doom picture

Chancel arch

Crucifix

Altar

Priest

Chancel

Nave

Porch with stoup of holy water

Font

The Cathedrals

In the Middle Ages England was divided into seventeen dioceses and each had a bishop at its head. A cathedral is the main church of a diocese. The word comes from the Latin word for throne, *cathedra*. Each cathedral had a bishop's throne, usually behind the high altar.

The bishop had enormous responsibilities, and for this he had about forty men to help him with the administration of the diocese. He was also landlord of the vast estates of his bishopric. But, most important, he regulated the practice of religion in as many as over a thousand parishes. Each autumn he held a synod, or meeting, of all the priests, and all year round he was obliged to travel to each of the parishes to make sure everyone was behaving properly. He held court and could fine, flog or excommunicate (deny all communion with the Church) people who had broken certain laws. Beyond this, many bishops had academic and cultural pursuits.

The cathedrals were usually built in towns. They were show-places and the product of

enormous spending on a scale which is hard to imagine today. It was here that medieval engineering technology was tried and tested.

In these days, before reinforced concrete, the walls of high buildings had to be supported by buttressing outside the walls to keep them from collapsing. This required the installation of huge stone supports which extended well beyond the sides of the buildings.

English cathedrals are distinguished by their very high spires. For example, the one at Lincoln reached a height of 548 feet (about 170 metres). Unfortunately it was destroyed in a storm in the sixteenth century and never replaced. But the one at Salisbury (1334) still stands, and the buckling of the walls beneath it testifies to the problems of excessive weight which the walls had to bear.

Like the altars in parish churches, the main altar of a cathedral is always in the east end of the building. English cathedrals are built on the cross-plan, so the spire is above the central crossing which had transepts, or arms, on either side. Many small chapels with altars are built along the aisles. As in some churches, many cathedrals have Lady Chapels dedicated to the Virgin Mary off the east end. A feature not found in parish churches, however, is the Chapter House. This is where the administration of the business of the diocese is conducted.

Seven English cathedrals were run by monks; these have cloisters or covered walkways surrounding a courtyard which led to the monks' living quarters.

The decoration that is part of so many of these great churches was designed to show Church teachings, but they are also very fine works of art. In the West Country, the Church authorities favoured sculpture, and several cathedrals are covered in rows of statues. In other areas, the stained glass windows served a similar educative purpose.

The complex theological presentation on the sculptural facade (top left) of Wells Cathedral (1230-55) begins at the top with Christ in Majesty; on either side of the centre are corresponding figures from the Old and New Testaments. Left, the strainer arch relieves the pressure of weight of the stone walls inside the crossing.

The fruit stealers on a capital in the south transept of Wells Cathedral (right) made about 1220 are about to learn an unsophisticated moral lesson when they are caught and punished. The 'stiff-leaf' foliage is characteristic of the Early English style.
Below, mason's marks, personal emblems carved onto the finished stones, identify the work of individual masons. Over 500 different marks have been identified at Wells.

Pilgrimage

People believed that saints had special powers which remained in their bodies long after their spirits had departed. Relics, the bones of saints, kept after their death, could cure illness, drive out demons and, when carried into battle, they could defeat the enemy. Objects placed near them grew heavier and the water which washed them took on their curing powers. Although saints could appear to the faithful in dreams, the real proof of saintliness was in the miracles performed by relics.

Relics of saints were highly prized, and distributed amongst churches or sold to individuals, and were then kept in a casket called a shrine. Those churches lucky enough to have noteworthy relics kept them in the holiest possible place, just east of the altar. They brought revenue to the church because people travelled great distances to benefit from them and left offerings for the saint.

A black market in relics soon arose. Gullible people paid large sums to gaze upon fake relics. Sometimes these were as unlikely as Christ's breath in a bottle or even the Devil's tail.

The reasons people went on pilgrimage varied: some were truly devout; others had to do penance, or an act of repentance, for some wrongdoing. They might wear sackcloth and ashes and walk for miles to be beaten by the attendant monks when they arrived. Probably the great majority of visitors to the shrines came for medical help.

Medieval medicine must have been frightening as well as ineffective. It included practices such as flebotomy (slicing veins open to drain off bad blood which caused illness) and cauterization (applying hot irons to parts of the body to relieve pain elsewhere).

Yet other people went on pilgrimage simply to have a good time. Palmers, for example, were professional pilgrims who, for a fee, would undertake pilgrimage for those who could not go themselves.

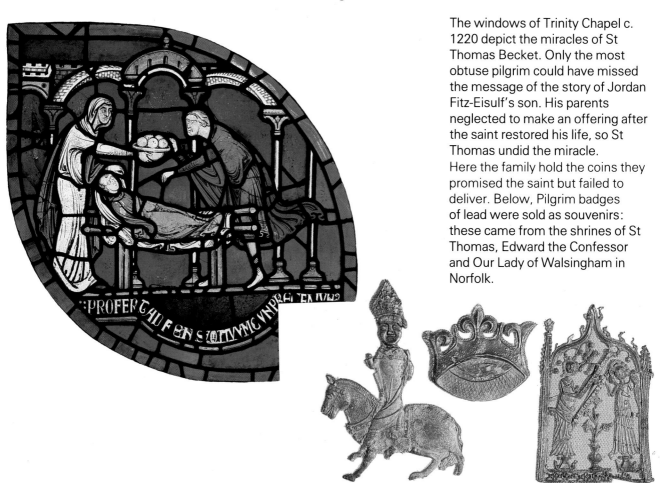

The windows of Trinity Chapel c. 1220 depict the miracles of St Thomas Becket. Only the most obtuse pilgrim could have missed the message of the story of Jordan Fitz-Eisulf's son. His parents neglected to make an offering after the saint restored his life, so St Thomas undid the miracle.

Here the family hold the coins they promised the saint but failed to deliver. Below, Pilgrim badges of lead were sold as souvenirs: these came from the shrines of St Thomas, Edward the Confessor and Our Lady of Walsingham in Norfolk.

Miracles recorded at the shrines indicate that pilgrims of different sex and status venerated different saints. The Saxon princess Frideswide, whose tomb was at Oxford, attracted middle and upper class women. Simon de Montfort, who had been excommunicated so never became a saint, worked miracles for many anti-royalists at his tomb in Evesham. Merchants in Norwich found a patron in the child saint, William, whom Jewish moneylenders were said to have murdered. By far the most celebrated cult was Thomas Becket's. His shrine in Canterbury was visited by pilgrims of all classes from all over Europe.

A miracle was defined by Thomas Aquinas as "anything that God did beyond the commonly observed in nature." Even the scientist Roger Bacon, who regarded most miracles with contempt, was pleased to note several. Theological arguments mattered little to most people who experienced miracles; the important thing was what the saints could do for them.

A carved roof boss from Exeter Cathedral of about 1350 shows the martyrdom of St Thomas Becket. He was praying in Canterbury Cathedral when he was murdered by two of Henry II's knights.

Below, in a picture from the *Life of Edward the Confessor*, a child leads seven blind men to the shrine of the Confessor. We see them again after they have been cured, with their hands raised in joy. Figures of a pilgrim, with purse, hat and staff, and of the Confessor stand on pedestals. The shrine of Edward the Confessor still exists at Westminster Abbey, which was re-built in the mid-13th century partly as a show place for his relics. It was also designed to be the Coronation church and the royal burial place.

Knowledge and Power

Knowledge

From the early Middle Ages the church held a monopoly on education. For centuries only monks actually needed to read. But from the twelfth century, written documents became increasingly a part of civilized life in government administration and in ordinary business. Because of this, ordinary people wanted to become literate. By 1300 practical literacy was common, not only for the nobility but for many others. However, education was still mainly only for boys. Even nuns, who had to be able to follow Latin texts, rarely acquired more than the most basic ability to recognize words and letters. Understanding and writing needed more education than was usually offered to women.

There were, for boys, several types of schools; most of them were only open to those who could afford them. Younger boys from seven to ten years old attended song schools to learn the ABC and to sing in the church choir. Peasant boys were occasionally taught by the village priest so they could serve at Mass. To go on to grammar school boys had to be able to read the Psalter, (book of Psalms), or the Hours of the Virgin, from the Book of Hours, and know the Lord's Prayer by heart.

In the thirteenth century universities independent of the Church were founded at Oxford and Cambridge to teach canon (Church) and civil law and theology (the study of religion). From the fourteenth century there was a new kind of practical education: business schools taught letter writing, accountancy, law and French, which was essential for legal matters.

English was becoming more important as an official language. After the mid-fourteenth century it became a normal part of schooling. Parliament was opened in English for the first time in 1363, and the Bible was translated into English in the 1380s.

The medieval educational system itself was based upon the way Aristotle's pupils classified his literary works. This resulted in the seven 'liberal arts', the 'humane studies'. Of these Grammar was the basic one, followed by Dialectic (the art of reasoning), and Rhetoric

This monkey school, which decorates the margins of a manuscript, exemplifies a kind of medieval humour. Animals 'aping' human behaviour was a favourite way of poking fun at those who took themselves too seriously – no one was above this treatment. Kings, clergy, and even funerals are portrayed by rabbits, geese and foxes (like those recreated in the chapter headings of this book). They can be found not only in books, but in woodcarving, and stained glass, and stone sculpture.

The chained library of the cathedral at Hereford is restored to look like it did in the Middle Ages. In monastic libraries monks or nuns would retire to the cloister every day to read from after the midday meal until Evensong. During Lent they were assigned one book for the year's reading, but not all of them managed to finish. Libraries began to keep book lists in the twelfth century. The friars devised indexes and made the first descriptive catalogues of books. They were also the first to loan books to readers.

(the ability to express that reasoning in an eloquent manner). The remaining four 'arts' – Arithmetic, Geometry, Music and Astronomy – were less systematically taught. They were usually very different from the modern version of the subjects. In theory seven 'mechanical arts' existed as well, embracing more practical subjects such as architecture and even 'art' in the modern sense.

Within the realm of higher education, theology was "queen of the sciences". The disciplines of philosophy and logic were the essential tools required to understand it, and for these medieval educators had always depended on Greek thinkers. Plato's works on the soul and faith and Aristotle's ideas of logic and science were adapted from the ancient Greek to the Christian culture. As one teacher expressed it, if scholars of the Middle Ages could see any further than those ancient philosophers it was because they were like dwarves standing on the shoulders of the giants of Antiquity.

In the thirteenth century many scientific and ethical writings by Aristotle and the works of Jewish and Arabic thinkers were translated into Latin. These ideas revolutionized the way people looked at the world and led towards the

Medieval books are hand-made objects from start to finish, and many specialist skills were involved in making them. First the *parchmenter* prepared the animal skin to make the pages. He stretched out the skins of sheep, goats or calves to dry and scraped the hair from them. These parchments were sold to the *scribes*, or writers, who cut them to size and ruled margins and lines for writing before beginning the laborious task of copying out the text. In larger workshops this job might be shared by several scribes to speed things up. If the book was to have decoration, the *illuminators* would then paint borders, gild the letters or paint pictures. The finished sheets were then passed to the *binder*, who sewed four sheets together in quires (or 16-page booklets). These quires were stitched together and enclosed in boards which were then covered in leather.

modern scientific method.

The advancement of knowledge in the Middle Ages depended on the availability of books, which were copied not printed. These were expensive because of the time, skilled labour and costs of the materials. In the earlier Middle Ages books were made by the people who used them, the monks. But by the thirteenth century increasing literacy moved book production to the market-place, where it remains today.

Literature: Innovation

As literacy spread from the clergy to lay people in the late Middle Ages, people began to read for entertainment. In the thirteenth century the nobility enjoyed adventure stories and romances in French. Legends of heroes, such as Alexander the Great who conquered the entire ancient world, provided the image of an ideal warrior hero. Slightly later stories, such as Tristan and Isolde, embodied the new sentiment of romantic love.

As English became the accepted national language in the fourteenth century, native writers produced the first great English literature for a wider audience. Most of this writing is steeped in religion and has a moral purpose. But writers such as Langland, who wrote *Piers Plowman*, did not hesitate to ridicule figures of authority. The characters often represent the voice of the new middle class. The needs for reform of religion and social institutions were underlying themes in Langland's writing.

The *Canterbury Tales* written by Geoffrey Chaucer from about 1387 onwards are the stories told by a group of pilgrims on their journey to Canterbury. The subtle portrayal of characters and their amusing and sometimes irreverent tales have provided entertainment for generations of readers.

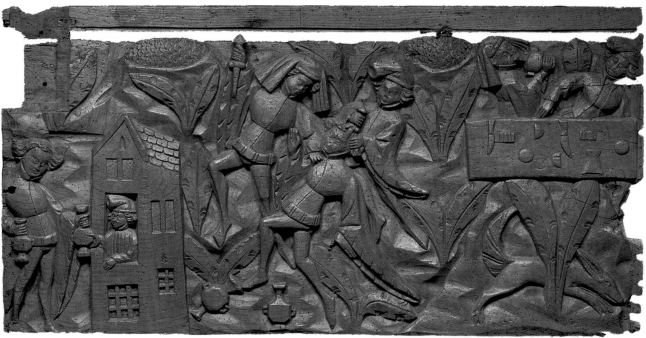

Reference Books: Tradition

The Bible, always the most important of all books, changed radically in format in response to ideas about how it should be read. Instructive commentaries were written in the margins and between the lines, so that a complete Bible could run to 22 volumes. Under the influence of the universities, this material was reduced to short prologues and hundreds of compact, single-volume Bibles were produced for scholars. The fourteenth-century translations into English and French extended the possibility of Bible reading to an even wider public.

People in the Middle Ages believed that nature reflected God's purpose. It is this belief that led to the unusual treatment of many subjects that we would consider sciences. Animals in the Bestiaries (or books about beasts) and stones in the Lapidaries (or books about stones) are described in terms of fable and magic. The *Marvels of the East* (translated from Greek) portrays foreign countries populated by people with only one leg, and men with dogs' heads. Herbals (books about plants), by contrast, were more practical; local plants used in the preparation of medicines are described in accurate detail. At his most characteristic, the medieval scholar was an organizer. He loved to build systems, make diagrams, and fit things into their proper places. Bartholomew the Englishman's encyclopedia is one of the earliest attempts to put universal knowledge into some form of order.

Alphabetical order was established around 1300. Before that, material was arranged according to its importance, beginning with God.

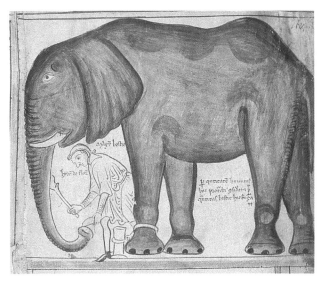

Two pictures of elephants by different artists illustrate the value of observation. Below, the blue Bestiary elephant with beak and claws, of about 1220, fights with a griffin. Above, Matthew Paris's elephant from *The Greater Chronicle* is more recognizable, for an elephant had been brought to England as a gift to the King. He even includes the keeper to indicate scale.

The banqueting scene from the romance of Lancelot du Lac (above left) was painted by English artists about 1350 over an earlier picture. The book was originally made in France. Note the apes in the bottom right hand corner.

The Pardoner's Tale chest of about 1400 (left) illustrates one of the *Canterbury Tales*. Death teaches three men who find a pot of gold a hard lesson about greed.

Science

For medieval people all the parts of the universe functioned together in a unified whole. The Earth was the fixed centre of a series of concentric circles in which the planets orbit, rising in the east and setting in the west. The Moon was the closest, followed by Mercury, Venus, the Sun, Mars, Jupiter, Saturn and the fixed stars. God and the nine orders of angels lived in the sphere beyond. Air extended all the way to the Moon's orbit; the rest of space was filled with a substance called *aether*. Demons appropriate to each planet lived in the aether. Hell was at the very centre below the Earth.

The planets affected life and substance on Earth. The light and warmth of the Sun were obvious, but more subtle 'celestial influences', created by movements of heavenly bodies, produced events and natural phenomena. Human will and intellect, with proper direction, could overcome evil effects. Astronomers studied the Heavens to learn more about the eternal order – whether the stars were animate creatures, whether God existed in the void

The invention of the weight-driven mechanical clock around 1300 revolutionized timekeeping; instead of dividing night and day into hours based on daylight, they came to be divided into 24 equal hours. The huge astronomical clock from St Albans is shown, left, by its creator, Abbot Righard of Walingford in a picture from the St Albans Book of Benefactors. The clock was 3.5 metres high, 3 metres wide and 1.5 metres deep and was hung on a wall. Manuscript drawings which survive show the complicated wheel works for a system which displayed the motions of the planets including the phases of the moon and tides. Richard was the son of a blacksmith, educated at Merton College, Oxford, who became the greatest mathematician of his day. The spots on his face are from leprosy, the disease from which he died.

Magic and science often used the same technology in the Middle Ages. The main difference is that the magic had a material end, while science is concerned with objective knowledge. The page shown above is from a manuscript about geomancy which was made for Richard II in about 1390. Geomancy is earth-magic. It is practised by a diviner who first makes a series of random dots in the earth and then looks up their astrological correspondance for the interpretation of fate.

beyond the planets – and also for more material and magical ends: to anticipate their Fate.

It was thought that there was a correspondence of feeling between earthly events and activity in outer space. Chaucer refers to the tides as the sea's 'desire' to follow the Moon. Roger Bacon describes the iron moving in 'sympathy' to the magnet. Since theology was queen of the sciences, spiritual matters were more important than physical ones and psychology (knowledge of the soul) was correspondingly more important than physical medicine. Man's rational soul set him above the beasts and just below the angels in the medieval hierarchy. The soul comes from and returns to God, all souls were created in splendour at the same time as the angels and their birth on this planet was cause for gloom. The soul had ten wits, the five inward wits – sight, hearing, smell, touch and taste – and five outward wits – memory, estimation, imagination, fantasy and common sense. The spirit holds the body and soul together; insanity shows the spirit is unwell.

The physical body, like all natural substances, was composed of four elements – earth, air, fire and water. These form the four humours – bile, phlegm, blood and choler – which in various combinations form temperaments and complexions. Medicine was based largely on the writings of Galen, a second century physician. Medical research did not exist – diagnosis and treatment were more important than understanding the causes and symptoms.

The reason that medieval science was so different from modern is that it was used for a different purpose. The underlying questions and techniques were aimed at proving the pre-eminence of God. This reliance upon authority narrowed people's horizons of thought. Still, it was the rediscovery of Aristotle's writings on philosophical and scientific subjects, along with Arab and Jewish writings on algebra and optics, that provided the impetus for a revolution in thinking. In the twelfth century, Adelard of Bath boldly separated natural from divine causes, and in the thirteenth century, Robert Grosseteste formulated the scientific method, based on objective observation of facts. He was also amongst the first to use mathematics to determine quantity rather than quality.

Today we place our faith in reason and take for granted the ideas of relating theories to observed facts, logically constructed arguments and experimental testing. For people in the Middle Ages, educated to use reason to prove faith, this represents an enormous mental leap and a great achievement.

After the Great Flood, in the time of Noah, God sent a rainbow as a sign of his promise never to destroy the Earth again. The rainbow was also an object of scientific inquiry. Robert Grosseteste, bishop of Lincoln, correctly identified refraction as an essential feature of it. Roger Bacon later proved that light shining on individual raindrops produces a different rainbow for each observer.

The Black Death

The Black Death (or Plague) originated in Central Asia in 1338 and spread first to China and India, then followed the trade routes to Europe, probably carried by the fleas which lived on rats in cargo ships, and arrived at a West Country port in 1349.

Victims of the bubonic plague were infected by insect-borne bacilli which caused huge swellings – buboes – to appear in armpit or groin. High fever, internal bleeding, and often insanity led to death in less than a week. Pulmonary plague could be passed on by coughing or simply breathing and was therefore potentially more deadly. Within two days the victim was dead. A third variant, septicaemic plague, was carried by fleas: it killed within hours, and victims could die in their sleep without even knowing they were infected.

Contemporary theories of the source of the menace varied. Some thought that it was transmitted by personal contact, either by touching or by visual contact. A myth arose which explained the mystery as a spirit in the form of a young girl who flew through the air. She emerged from the mouths of the dead plague victims as a blue flame.

More scientific theories centred on atmospheric or planetary influence. One scientist blamed the eruption of poisonous gases from an earthquake. The medical faculty of the University of Paris decided that an evil conjunction of Jupiter, Saturn and Mars which had occurred in 1345 was at fault. Only one contemporary doctor distinguished between the bubonic and pulmonary varieties; not even he knew what to do about it.

A fatalistic reaction, typified by Langland's "these pestilences were for pure sin", was the commonplace attitude. The Bishop of Winchester imposed penances on his people in the hope that salvation of their souls might also save their bodies. But even though the inhabitants of his diocese recited Psalms and prayers and walked barefoot around the market-place three times a week, the result was hardly encouraging. The Black Death was especially cruel to Winchester where 49 per cent of the clergy alone died.

Medieval hygiene was deplorable. The cities were overcrowded, raw sewage was dumped into the streets and even in wealthier households many people slept in the same room. In the countryside livestock was commonly kept in the houses along with the families. The fleas and rats which carried the terrible disease must

have been part of everyday life at the time.

By 1350 the Black Death had run its course in Britain and fully one out of every three people had died. Such a catastrophe could not fail to affect social and religious institutions and attitudes. Everyone in the country was personally affected; everyone would certainly have known at least one person who had perished from the Plague.

The Church anticipated the resurrection of the dead on Judgement Day, so burials had to be in consecrated ground. So many people died in 1349 that new churchyards often had to be found, and many corpses had to be left in common pits. Scenes such as this from a Flemish chronicle would also have been commonplace in England.

Index

Note: page numbers in *italics* refer to illustrations